Writer's Idea Journal

COPYRIGHT © 2022
Writer's Idea Journal
by R.W. Jensen

NOTICE OF COPYRIGHT

All rights reserved. No part of this book may be reproduced or transmitted in any form or by any means, electronic or mechanical, including photo copying, recording or by an information storage and retrieval system without permission of the author, except from the inclusion of brief quotations in a review. Even though this is mainly a blank notebook the silly laws force us to list a copyright page.

First Printing Edition, 2022

Paperback ISBN: 978-1-954253-11-7
Hardback ISBN: 978-1-954253-12-4

Blank Pages

Use these to command the page

- **Cover** doodles and ideas.
- **Chapter Start Art** curlicues and other ideas for your chapter art.
- **Write** Tall and Large to show off great ideas.
- **Free Form** writing.

Elements of Writing

Use these to decide your Genre/Topic for each day

- **Names** of people and places to reflect the tone you want to set.

- **Character** types, ways to develop each character.

- **Dialog:** write down good lines – there will be a character coming along to claim that brilliance in this book or the next.

- **Plot:** over plot ideas or small side plot ideas.

- **Audience:** different niche audiences for your books.

- **Your Bio Page:** write ideas, you can have a different bio for each book.

- **Cover Thoughts:** elements or full cover ideas.

- **Physical:** settings or people, describe it as you want a reader to see it.

- **Theme:** connected feelings, words, ideas, grammar structures to pull your theme together.

- **Point of View:** Your thoughts on how to play around with a POV for different chapters.

- **Vocabulary:** List favorite or powerful words you will want to use.

- **The When/Where:** historical periods, current places – write down striking times and places you can bring to life.

- **Random:** Never forgot the treasure in a random thought that can be used now or perhaps guarded until the right time … write it down so it is not lost to the shadows of memory.

Idea of the Day:

Date: *Genre/Topic:*

Idea of the Day:

Date: *Genre/Topic:*

Idea of the Day:

Date: *Genre/Topic:*

Idea of the Day:

Date: *Genre/Topic:*

Idea of the Day:

Date: *Genre/Topic:*

Idea of the Day:

Date: *Genre/Topic:*

Idea of the Day:

Date: *Genre/Topic:*

Idea of the Day:

Date: *Genre/Topic:*

Idea of the Day:

Date: *Genre/Topic:*

Idea of the Day:

Date: *Genre/Topic:*

Idea of the Day:

Date: *Genre/Topic:*

Idea of the Day:

Date: *Genre/Topic:*

Idea of the Day:

Date: *Genre/Topic:*

Idea of the Day:

Date: *Genre/Topic:*

Idea of the Day:

Date: *Genre/Topic:*

Idea of the Day:

Date: *Genre/Topic:*

Idea of the Day:

Date: *Genre/Topic:*

Idea of the Day:

Date: *Genre/Topic:*

Idea of the Day:

Date: *Genre/Topic:*

Idea of the Day:

Date: *Genre/Topic:*

Idea of the Day:

Date: *Genre/Topic:*

Idea of the Day:

Date: *Genre/Topic:*

Idea of the Day:

Date: *Genre/Topic:*

Idea of the Day:

Date: *Genre/Topic:*

Idea of the Day:

Date: *Genre/Topic:*

Idea of the Day:

Date: *Genre/Topic:*

Idea of the Day:

Date: *Genre/Topic:*

Idea of the Day:

Date: *Genre/Topic:*

Idea of the Day:

Date: *Genre/Topic:*

Idea of the Day:

Date: *Genre/Topic:*

Idea of the Day:

Date: *Genre/Topic:*

Idea of the Day:

Date: *Genre/Topic:*

Idea of the Day:

Date: *Genre/Topic:*

Idea of the Day:

Date: *Genre/Topic:*

Idea of the Day:

Date: *Genre/Topic:*

Idea of the Day:

Date: *Genre/Topic:*

Idea of the Day:

Date: *Genre/Topic:*

Idea of the Day:

Date: *Genre/Topic:*

Idea of the Day:

Date: *Genre/Topic:*

Idea of the Day:

Date: *Genre/Topic:*

Idea of the Day:

Date: *Genre/Topic:*

Idea of the Day:

Date: *Genre/Topic:*

Idea of the Day:

Date: *Genre/Topic:*

Idea of the Day:

Date: *Genre/Topic:*

Idea of the Day:

Date: *Genre/Topic:*

Idea of the Day:

Date: *Genre/Topic:*

Idea of the Day:

Date: *Genre/Topic:*

Idea of the Day:

Date: *Genre/Topic:*

Idea of the Day:

Date: *Genre/Topic:*

Idea of the Day:

Date: *Genre/Topic:*

Idea of the Day:

Date: *Genre/Topic:*

Idea of the Day:

Date: *Genre/Topic:*

Idea of the Day:

Date: *Genre/Topic:*

Idea of the Day:

Date: *Genre/Topic:*

Idea of the Day:

Date: *Genre/Topic:*

Idea of the Day:

Date: *Genre/Topic:*

Idea of the Day:

Date: *Genre/Topic:*

Idea of the Day:

Date: *Genre/Topic:*

Idea of the Day:

Date: *Genre/Topic:*

Idea of the Day:

Date: *Genre/Topic:*

Idea of the Day:

Date: *Genre/Topic:*

Idea of the Day:

Date: *Genre/Topic:*

Idea of the Day:

Date: *Genre/Topic:*

Idea of the Day:

Date: *Genre/Topic:*

Idea of the Day:

Date: *Genre/Topic:*

Idea of the Day:

Date: *Genre/Topic:*

Idea of the Day:

Date: *Genre/Topic:*

Idea of the Day:

Date: *Genre/Topic:*

Idea of the Day:

Date: *Genre/Topic:*

Idea of the Day:

Date: *Genre/Topic:*

Idea of the Day:

Date: *Genre/Topic:*

Idea of the Day:

Date: *Genre/Topic:*

Idea of the Day:

Date: *Genre/Topic:*

Idea of the Day:

Date: *Genre/Topic:*

Idea of the Day:

Date: *Genre/Topic:*

Idea of the Day:

Date: *Genre/Topic:*

Idea of the Day:

Date: *Genre/Topic:*

Idea of the Day:

Date: *Genre/Topic:*

Idea of the Day:

Date: *Genre/Topic:*

Idea of the Day:

Date: *Genre/Topic:*

Idea of the Day:

Date: *Genre/Topic:*

Idea of the Day:

Date: *Genre/Topic:*

Idea of the Day:

Date: *Genre/Topic:*

Idea of the Day:

Date: *Genre/Topic:*

Idea of the Day:

Date: *Genre/Topic:*

Idea of the Day:

Date: *Genre/Topic:*

_____
_____
_____

_____
_____
_____
_____
_____
_____
_____
_____
_____
_____
_____

Idea of the Day:

Date: Genre/Topic:

Idea of the Day:

Date: *Genre/Topic:*

Idea of the Day:

Date: *Genre/Topic:*

Idea of the Day:

Date: *Genre/Topic:*

Idea of the Day:

Date: *Genre/Topic:*

Idea of the Day:

Date: *Genre/Topic:*

Idea of the Day:

Date: *Genre/Topic:*

Idea of the Day:

Date: *Genre/Topic:*

Idea of the Day:

Date: *Genre/Topic:*

Idea of the Day:

Date: *Genre/Topic:*

Idea of the Day:

Date: *Genre/Topic:*

Idea of the Day:

Date: *Genre/Topic:*

Idea of the Day:

Date: *Genre/Topic:*

Idea of the Day:

Date: *Genre/Topic:*

Idea of the Day:

Date: *Genre/Topic:*

Idea of the Day:

Date: *Genre/Topic:*

Idea of the Day:

Date: *Genre/Topic:*

Idea of the Day:

Date: *Genre/Topic:*

Idea of the Day:

Date: *Genre/Topic:*

Idea of the Day:

Date: *Genre/Topic:*

Idea of the Day:

Date: *Genre/Topic:*

Idea of the Day:

Date: *Genre/Topic:*

Idea of the Day:

Date: *Genre/Topic:*

Idea of the Day:

Date: *Genre/Topic:*

Idea of the Day:

Date: *Genre/Topic:*

Idea of the Day:

Date: *Genre/Topic:*

Idea of the Day:

Date: *Genre/Topic:*

Idea of the Day:

Date: *Genre/Topic:*

Idea of the Day:

Date: *Genre/Topic:*

Idea of the Day:

Date: *Genre/Topic:*

Idea of the Day:

Date: *Genre/Topic:*

Idea of the Day:

Date: *Genre/Topic:*

Idea of the Day:

Date: *Genre/Topic:*

Idea of the Day:

Date: *Genre/Topic:*

Idea of the Day:

Date: *Genre/Topic:*

Idea of the Day:

Date: *Genre/Topic:*

Idea of the Day:

Date: *Genre/Topic:*

Idea of the Day:

Date: *Genre/Topic:*

Idea of the Day:

Date: *Genre/Topic:*

Idea of the Day:

Date: *Genre/Topic:*

Idea of the Day:

Date: *Genre/Topic:*

Idea of the Day:

Date: *Genre/Topic:*

Idea of the Day:

Date: *Genre/Topic:*

Idea of the Day:

Date: *Genre/Topic:*

Idea of the Day:

Date: *Genre/Topic:*

Idea of the Day:

Date: *Genre/Topic:*

Idea of the Day:

Date: *Genre/Topic:*

Idea of the Day:

Date: *Genre/Topic:*

Idea of the Day:

Date: *Genre/Topic:*

Idea of the Day:

Date: *Genre/Topic:*

Idea of the Day:

Date: *Genre/Topic:*

Idea of the Day:

Date: *Genre/Topic:*

Idea of the Day:

Date: *Genre/Topic:*

Idea of the Day:

Date: *Genre/Topic:*

Idea of the Day:

Date:　　　　　　　　　　　　　　　*Genre/Topic:*

Idea of the Day:

Date: *Genre/Topic:*

Idea of the Day:

Date: *Genre/Topic:*

Idea of the Day:

Date: *Genre/Topic:*

Idea of the Day:

Date: *Genre/Topic:*

Idea of the Day:

Date: *Genre/Topic:*

Idea of the Day:

Date: *Genre/Topic:*

Idea of the Day:

Date: *Genre/Topic:*

Idea of the Day:

Date: *Genre/Topic:*

Idea of the Day:

Date: *Genre/Topic:*

Idea of the Day:

Date: *Genre/Topic:*

Idea of the Day:

Date: *Genre/Topic:*

Dear Reader and Writer:

Now that you have put in so much work – you understand how ALL New Authors work hard – consider buying a book from Van Velzer Press – this is a publisher who is woman-owned, veteran friendly and independent – Van Velzer Press works hard to give new authors a way to get their books out there and gives them generous help, support and a royalty breakdown that none of the big houses offer any but their best and proven authors.

Visit the website:

Vanvelzerpress.com

Thank you and I hope you feel creative and inspired after finishing this journal !

~ R. W. Jensen

www.ingramcontent.com/pod-product-compliance
Lightning Source LLC
Chambersburg PA
CBHW081346070526
44578CB00005B/736